Just To Spend A Little Time

With You!

[A Lifetime of Writing Poetry]

BY
JAMES MONROE JOHNSON

ISBN: 1-4107-6071-5 (e-book)
ISBN: 1-4107-6070-7 (Paperback)

This book is printed on acid free paper.

1stBooks – rev. 6/26/03

All the writings in this work have no existence outside the imagination of the author, and have no relations whatsoever to anyone bearing the same name or names, resemblances and/or nicknames. However, all of this work is inspired by persons, both personally known or casually acquainted, by the author and all incidents depicted in these writings are based solely on the pure imaginary inventions of the author.

The Author

DEDICATION

To the many devoted friends and acquaintances, relatives, former teachers and college instructors, university professors and friendly pundits who have seen, read and studied my work over the years, I dedicate this series of personal imaginary processes of poetic thought to each of you with the hope and prayers that you wholeheartedly approve.

James Monroe Johnson

FOREWORD

To make it easily understandable — to the reader — each poem is titled, dated, and labeled with the location where it was written. In most cases, the place where the poem was written will say, most vividly to those that know me well exactly what I was doing. In other words, if the poem was written in Da Nang, South Vietnam, those that know me will readily know that I was in the Army, and that I was fighting the war as a soldier, and not as an administrator for some governmental agency, or some other private company.

I started writing poems and other poetic verses and phrases as far back as I can remember, but only through the encouragement of teachers did I began to save my writings. Thusly, the first recorded poem was in 1962, a song for a band I played with in college.

Over the years, my writings have given hope, inspiration and liveliness to others, as well as tons of insightful memories to me, and hopefully, these poems will reach countless others and bring some laughter, hope, inspiration and joy to their lives. That is the purpose of my writing.

I have written songs for choirs, gospel groups and individuals, some of which have been set to music, recorded and copywrited.

If you look closer, the average reader can sense the changes in my life through my writings, from the do-nothing attitudes through the it's-mine-or-else selfishness to the I-love-you-in-spite-of-yourself idea. Those of you that find only intrigue, or laughter in those areas that are not fully comprehensible, it is safe to note that I will be laughing with you, for I, as the author, was often intrigued, and even lost at some of my own writings.

Here's hoping you find something of value in my poems.

TABLE OF CONTENTS

"About Me"
(June 29, 1974)
Miami, Florida

I am me
A black, a man
I was a black before I was a man
I am tall, light and tan
not slim or heavy
but moderate to medium

I am educated
slightly, common sensical
artistic and poetic, instinctively

I am multi-talented
southern born and idealistically bred
extrovertedly outspoken

I dress, originally
have creative thoughts, am an injured humanitarian
I am such sometimes moody
seldom emotional, abruptly romantic
and French-oriented

I have many thoughts, few ideas
envious of nobody, jealous of on one
follower of few
leader of none

I identify with everybody
but I am me, a realist and a dreamer
and now
you think you know me!

JAMES MONROE JOHNSON

"Fall Heir To Kindness"
(April 5, 1967)
Fort Campbell, Kentucky

When he speaks, in a soft melodic tone
beware the would, dear lady, beware;
where his paws touch are left bewildered
avoid his eyes and their subtle stare

Walking as light as a one-feathered fowl
stalking prey after prey, he behooves the lot;
one strike of the paw at a delicate jaw
the victim lies conquered and she knows not

Appearing placently, he is overly smooth
but he is a wolf from deep within;
seeming shy, he's determinedly sly
fall heir to kindness, he doth win

He is bold, he is brazen and he is hasty
he thinks advantageously for himself;
he has caused many a deep pain endurance
hear not his woes, his words are death

Fall, dear lady, but beware the path
fall enviously into the pool of charms;
let none other speak of kindness to you
'cause you've fallen heir to my arms

Fall heir to kindness, dear lady, fall deeply
and dream erotically when you sleep;
I am the eyes of your knight of honor
I watch over you when you weep

I speak against the devil, he who dares
to touch that of mine in happiness yet;
now I speak of you, if you must fall
fall heir to kindness and have no regret!

JAMES MONROE JOHNSON

"Conviction of Failure"
(November 7, 1969)
Pleiku, South Vietnam

Arrest me for conspiracy
I'm as guilty as the law defines
jail me for my participation
I know these feelings of mine

Arraign me for my actions
I can't claim a bit on innocence
indict me for contempt of beliefs
my energy in faith is spent

Try me for liking the damages
that my open stupidity caused
convict me of basic human frailties
shoot me continually until I fall

Sentence me for my emotions
prosecute me for my sneaky game
throw me over into the lion's den
please don't spare me any pains

You've caught me, persecuted me
'n threw me unmercifully into your jail
think not only of the evil I've done
remember also it was I who failed!

"A Wishful Thought"
(July 10, 1965)
Fort Campbell, Kentucky

Someday I'll be happy when you're sad
'cause now I am miserable and you're glad;
you know a secret that's mine to be
but, for some reason, you won't tell me!

Yesterday, you wished me lots of luck
now you're telling me to give it up;
my mind is made with not a bit of doubt
I'll never give you up: I may give out!

Thoughts of you remind me of happy times
when you were with me, your hand in mine;
even now, when those times are past
I'm yet hoping the feelings will last!

My stars are out, my skies are blue
I sit here alone with sweet thoughts of you;
standing at the end of a very happy time
when I tried very much to make you mine!

Even now, I feel it still may go
you said you didn't believe I was jiving anymore;
that when I said something, you believe it true
'cause I'll always be here waiting for you!

JAMES MONROE JOHNSON

"To Say The Least"
(September 7, 1968)
Qui Nhon, South Vietnam

I admire you for your kindness, I do
I adore you for having the quality in you
I idolize your beauty for it being so true
to say the least: I envy you!

I hate your enemy, should there be one
I love your friends, they must be fun
I'm jealous of him when the evenings come
to say the least: I envy you!

I console your sadness as it stands
I pity your aggressor if he's a man
I see the work done by your hands
to say the least: I envy you!

I loathe the house in which you wed
I despise the doctor who'll pronounce you dead
I pursue the course of life you've led
to say the least: I envy you!

Of all the things that I could do
more than all, I want to be like you
many a lie I've told, but this is true
I'll say no more, but "I envy you!"

"Looking Back Into The Future"
(November 12, 1969)
Pleiku, South Vietnam

Of all the things I would rather do
    the most important would surely be
        that I could instill some faith in you
            and have you put some faith in me

Of all the many things I have done
    the most memorable would surely be
        that I could write another poem to you
            and have you send another note to me

Of all the things that I have said
    the most regrettable has to be
        the day I told myself that I didn't care
            that you developed feelings for me

Now, it's past and cannot be re-done
    like a lost battle that cannot be won
        what's turned in unhappiness that began as fun
            are the things of the past I've said and done!

"Because Of You"
(July 8, 1993)
Starkville, Mississippi

You called, I came running, you conquered
I hoped you were glad I came
through my writings you knew me
and you also saw the pain

If I found that root, and the cause
would I then find the pain?
is it yet possible for me to know
and would anything really change?

I'll have you know that I'm not happy
so be you not misled by my style
I am somewhat afraid to know
and it shows through my smile

When you called, I came quickly
and you conquered rapidly as well
though it is not in my repertoire
so I would certainly never tell

Now when I look back, I see clearly
certain things then in the rough
and I am beyond the stage of knowing
which makes it extremely tough

Moreover, I am yet worthy
and what I say, I always do
I am troubled only by my failure
and it's all because of you!

"Do, But Don't"
(July 30, 1968)
Saigon, South Vietnam

Fight your fears, girl
but don't fear the fight!

Right your wrong-doings
but don't wrong your rights!

Use your head, girl
but don't head its use!

Abuse your tormentors
but don't torment your abuse!

Take your time, girl
but don't time your takings!

Make your own
but don't own your makings!

Live your own life
but don't love your living!

Give your whole part
but don't part your givings!

Man your heart
but harden not your man!

Stand-up for your rights
and always right your stand!

JAMES MONROE JOHNSON

"Apologies Not Long"
(October 18, 1993)
Dallas, Texas

I ain't no Angel
Holy, I don't claim
    like all living things
    I also suffer pain
and when I have done wrong
it doesn't take me long......
...to apologize!

I ain't never been a bigshot
never claimed to be a saint
    there're some things
    I can do
    and some things I can't
but when I've done wrong
it's never taken me long...
...to apologize!

I haven't always been good
but real evil I never was
    though my religion is
    suspect
    I do believe in God
so when I've done a wrong
I make sure it ain't too long...
...to apologize!

I am only human
flesh and blood and bones
    I ain't gonna be here
    forever
    'cause life ain't promised
    long
that's why when I've done
wrong
I act before the feelings
are gone......
......to apologize!

Ain't never lived on a
pedestal
barely lived above a fool
    as a boy, had no choice
    was forced to go to
    school
    where I learned that
    when I've done wrong
    to make sure it doesn't
    take me long...
...to apologize!

I ain't responsible for everything
just those dumb things I do
and I am very much aware
of what I did to you
I know I have done you wrong
and I hope I haven't been too long...
...in apologizing!

"On The Borderline"
(August 5, 1974)
Racine, Wisconsin

On the borderling, I stood
a long time
borrowing time, borrowing many things
of worldly sorrow
of bad, and good, and sometimes distasteful
disgraceful and distraught
but nevertheless
borrowed

the good lasted not long
the bad lasted awhile longer
but the unsecure
the unknown
lasted but forever, and is still lasting
and lasting, and lasting......
......on the borderline

lasting is the thoughts
of the days gone past
times that couldn't last
things that would stand
from one day to another
but the memories
live on and on
if only in one mind
and for no real purpose
but the remembrance
of those things
that were
of those times

that were
and those people
that made it...be as it was
......on the borderline

"Love Is Giving"
(April 23, 1985
Pascagoula, Mississippi

What you don't ask
that I give
accept it and smile
use it and live

What I give to you
from my charitable heart
is forever yours to cherish
or wholly tear apart

What I continue
to give to you
implies in no way
what you should do

What you feel
plays little part
in what I give
from my heart

I will give to you
as long as you're living
for as long as I love
I will keep on giving!

"The Winged One"
(October 20, 1969)
Saigon, South Vietnam

Allow me to pass...
　　　　o'er the broken twig
a toast of kindness to great fair play;

　　does the big bird fly...
　　　　　　'cause he's too lazy to trod
or, is that his chosen way?

　　Why is the twig broken...
　　　　　　and to where did it flee?
sublety was it's great asset:

　　does the winged one flap...
　　　　　for lack of speed
or, is his soul obsessed?

　　A stone fallen on the bush
　　　　　and snapped went the twig
flailing slowing to the surfaced soil;

　　does the big bird land...
　　　　　'cause its journey is complete
or, does it's wing need oil?

O'er thousands of miles.........
　　　　the twig is lost
miles are ladened on the deep blue;

the winged one has landed.........
　　　　and its full-speed ahead
　　　　　　and it's all because of you!

14

"Love As Love Is"
(May 2, 1979)
Gautier, Mississippi

Love: A break-up of emotions
A complete break-down of attitudes;
A new rejuvenation of ideals......
...such is love as I know it!

Love: The completeness of caring
The absolute inference of sharing;
The utmost of basic human desires
... such is love in my life!

Love: The beauty of being together
The feeling of gratitude for oneself;
And those by which contact is made......
......such is love as I wish it to be!

Love: An everlasting thought of endearment
Superlative thoughts deep within;
And an abundance of teardrops.........
......that flows to no end.........

Such is Love as Love is!

JAMES MONROE JOHNSON

"My Love, You Are, I give"
(February 23, 1968)
Qui Nhon, South Vietnam

You are so lovely, you are so sweet
      the best of everything a guy could meet
to have, to hold for an everyday treat
      my love, you are, I give!

None more beautiful have I ever seen
      with more answers to any one man's dreams
with far more personality, by any means
      you are, my live, I give!

A face of glory, a body of faith
      any more qualities I couldn't take
I hope, in you, I've found my fate
      my love, you are, I give!

May God bless you for your smile
      for having in you, a beautiful child
I hope to make your time worthwhile
      you are, my love, I give!

"I Am But Not Am I"
(October 24, 1969)
Da Nang, South Vietnam

In a divided world, I live
in a complicated bliss

as all the while I ponder
the love back home I miss

Moreover, I am among many thousands
striving to preserve Freedom's Call

little I realize that here I am
but I'm not here at all

I work daily in one world, lonely
to retire, nightly, to my lonely room

eleven months more of such loneliness
in this world of devastating gloom

But, on the other side, also I am
yet, only part of me sustains reprieve

I didn't leave my heart in San Francisco
I didn't have a heart to leave!

JAMES MONROE JOHNSON

"The Sinner's Way"
(October 10, 1969)
Pleiku, South Vietnam

May God Bless —
            This Earthly Mess —
And May He Save —
            His Ungodly Slaves

                        May He Find —
                                    Peace of Mind —
                        O'er A Land —
                                    Of A Sinful Man

            May God Feel —
                        When I kneel —
            And Rest My Soul —
                        Of A Prayer Told

                        May He Rests —
                                    In His Sleep —
                        To Bury The Mighty
            Who harms the Meek

May He Arise —
            With Open Eyes —
                        On That Mornin' —
            I Hear The Horn

                        May God See —
                                    The Good In Me —
                        And Rest My Head —
                                    On A Hallowed Bed.

                                    AMEN!

"Just To Spend A Little Time With You"
(September 11, 1968)
Fort Benning, Georgia

I have never seen another
of anything that I wanted so bad
but just the thought of you
makes me feel so glad

and if I thought there ever were a way
that's the course I would gladly take

…just to spend a little time with you!

If I saw you walking down the streets
coming toward, or going away from me
I could change my stride and follow your way
and follow every step that you would take

and if I thought there were ever a way
that's the one I would gladly take

……just to spend a little time with you!

If I thought you whispered to me
and I didn't see your lips when you spoke
I would rush to your side and say hello
and wait for you to say much mo'

and if I thought there ever were a way
that's the direction that I would take

…………just to spend a little time with you!

19

"War Is Hell!"
(October 24, 1969)
Pleiku, South Vietnam

The valleys are full of the enemy
    the fields are bedded in rice
the tables are set with c-rations
    and my clothes are eaten by mice

Leeches are clinging onto my body
    mosquitoes are humming like bees
my boots are torn from sharpened bamboo
    and snakes are striking from trees

Ants are building huge mounds and hills
    scorpions are settling for one good bite
my ankles are swollen from lack of air
    from sleeping in my boots at night

My face is scratched and scarred to hell
    my arms and legs are full of rash
my head is shaven 'cause hair won't grow
    and on my forehead is a bayonet gash

These are some of the things, to name a few
    by being a soldier, I have to pull through
I pray to God to please let it be
    that I can live to face the enemy

It's not only the enemy that a soldier dreads
    it's the crawling creatures around his bed
if it weren't for prayer that set my pace
    I would've already given up my space

If anyone says something good about this war
hear not his words and bid him farewell
unless you've been here, you'll never know
the things we go through, 'cause WAR IS HELL!

JAMES MONROE JOHNSON

"What Is Your Pledge, Dear Luv?"
(September 1969)
Qui Nhon, South Vietnam

A fear of love is a fear of living
   there isn't life without love
to sacrifice one is abusing the other
  what is your pledge, dear luv?

Isn't there a desire: A desperate need?
   a longing for your heart to feed?
why torture yourself by your own creed?
  what is your pledge, dear luv?

The past is over, done and forgotten
   you must know "all men aren't rotten"
you're driving yourself; nerves on edge
  stop, dear luv: What is your pledge?

The likes of one don't motivate two
   'cause one man deliberately mistreated you
doesn't mean that I have to follow too
  what is your pledge, dear luv?

Drop the barrier from around your heart
   allow yourself to mend the broken part
permit me to give your love a new start
  what is your pledge, dear luv?

You can't live forever in isolation
   eventually you'll miss love's adoration
that comes in a man-woman association
  what is your pledge, dear luv?

I shall await some answer from you
        to see if my words are breaking through
that you've decided to turn your heart loose
    whatever is your pledge, dear luv?

"Already Got The Heart"
(April 14, 1985)
Moss Point, Mississippi

To you, I offer:
>consolation when you need it
>advice if you'll heed it
>my ego if you'll feed it

...'cause you have my heart already!

To you, I will be:
>a friend in the beginning
>salvation if you are sinning
>hoorahs while you are winning

......'cause you have my heart already!\

For you, I give:
>confidence to be sure
>morality to remain pure
>courage to endure

......'cause you have my heart already!

From you, I want:
>objectivity so I'll believe
>reciprocity so I'll achieve
>compatibility so I can conceive

......what's in my heart already!

"A Situation Baffled"
(April 23, 1985)
Moss Point, Mississippi

There's nothing I've ever done wrong
for which I didn't apologize
except those few things I did
that I didn't even realize

Very few things I have done
that I have lived to regret
unlike that unforgettable evening
when you and I first met

There's little I've ever said
that I've never really meant
except when my head buried my heart
and I wondered where it went

Only a place or two I've gone
that I wanted not to be
nothing have I ever seen
that I really didn't want to see

but, here's a situation that's got me baffled
and I really don't know what to do
is that day you said you couldn't love me
but you knew that I loved you!

JAMES MONROE JOHNSON

"An Island of Togetherness"
(July 6, 1974)
Key West, Florida

Let us come together

hand in hand

my thoughts become yours
if only you can feel

here I am beside you

so tenderly, so close

seeing you and believing
yes, we are real

while we are together
let not the sunsets pass

over the blue horizon yonder
our closeness continues to last

let us remain

together, as one
for happiness and fun

and all that life allows
to separate us

would destroy the cause
for which we stand

and destruct our mutual vows………

then, the little lady smiled
and said:

"Don't be critical of me!"

"If You Do Those Things"
(August 5, 1974)
Racine, Wisconsin

If you do those things
and I see them
am I to ignore that they're being done?

Or, do I have the right
to do those same things
or other things similar of my choosing?

If you have done those things
and I have known them
am I to believe my knowledge, or believe you?

Or, do I have rights equal
that I, too, may undertake the same
or having done them, am I still the equal?

Now that I know those things you do
do you stop doing them
or just pretend
or let me do those very same things too?

If you are through
doing those things you have done
and if I haven't started
will you hold it against me
if I try and catch up
by beginning now
with you?

"In Deep Thoughts Of You"
(May 29, 1968)
Fort Benning, Georgia

As I sit here, thinking, on the job each day
thoughts of you are forever blurring my way
no more work will I ever be able to do
as long as I'm sitting here — thinking of you

Each day gets longer, more unbearable all the time
each hour get more intolerable with you on my mind
thoughts of you are sweet, but oh, how they hurt
thinking of you all the time and never doing my work

It's so difficult to be side-tracked and working too
and that, my dear, is the only thinking that I do
about you, me, me, you, and things I wish for us
I adhere now to say, o Lord, give me love or bust

But, how sweet it is, to think of you
I can't think of anything else that I'd rather do
I sleep with dreams of your thinking of me, too
how beautiful is the world when I'm thinking of you......

......but I don't get much work done!

JAMES MONROE JOHNSON

"Oh! That Feeling!"
(November 11, 1967)
Qui Nhon, South Vietnam

Have you ever had a feeling?
And you didn't want it, but it was there?
For awhile you were so afraid of it
but soon realized you just didn't care?

You can't describe that feeling, really…
Just that it's thrilling and it hurts so deep
everything you do, that feeling stays with you
afraid to cry and ashamed to weep

You wish you could stop that painful feeling
it's affecting you in every way
but you think if you lost it, it's gone forever
so you have it now and you want it to stay

You're getting lazy, drowsy, and you can't eat
at night you read because you can't sleep
that feeling is with you and you're growing weak
and you slur every word you try to speak

What is that feeling you're having now?
The feeling you haven't had for so very long?
but, take my advice and take advantage of it
for if you don't, it'll soon be gone

And, if you're afraid of that feeling, don't be
even if it makes you feel so blue
you are not alone with that feeling
'cause I am having that feeling too!

JAMES MONROE JOHNSON

"A Touch Of Loneliness"
(December 28, 1969)
Qui Nhon, South Vietnam

Lonely I am, in misery, I must be
pains in my heart
will not release me

deep and emotional thoughts
are mine
to have
to hold
forever be

I feel, though I am lonely
yet I am
many miles of loneliness separates me

from the feel
of your warmth and kindness

a touch of loneliness
beckons me

I fell deeply
into the likes of you

and I pray
sincerely
for your best

If thoughts of me are with me
I know

you, too, feel
a touch of loneliness

I am lonesome without conquest
I feel only a touch of loneliness!

"May God Bless......"
(August 1, 1968)
Saigon, South Vietnam

May God bless
> the parents
> that love their little child

May His love
> abide with them
> that keeps it reconciled

May God bless
> the adults that watches
> over it as it grows

And share His love
> and blessings
> until its age is old

May God bless
> the student
> that keeps his rightful way

May He watch
> his every step forward
> until he can man his say

May God Bless
> the young lady
> that goes forth with the time

but may He curse and damn her
that can't make up her mind!

"Need I Say More?"
(October 19, 1969)
Qui Nhon, South Vietnam

Whatever the mood
you're an integral part
whatever the feeling
it's from the heart

wherever it goes
you're the one who starts
whenever the embrace
your arms will disembark

Let it be known to you
regardless of what you do
be advised that my honesty
doesn't always stand true

but everything I say
I'm prepared to follow through
Whatever the direction
your hand set the course

however wild the winds
you're its driving force
whenever I feel the urge
you'll never feel remorse

wherever I wish to go
it'll be with you, of course
However difficult the times
you could be the very cause

however tall I stand
you could easily make me fall
no matter how sad I am
I would worry none at all

Need I say more, dear lady
I can't find a better cause!

"A Better Day Tomorrow"
(July 7, 1993)
Starkville, Mississippi

In my life is some sorrow
      sometimes, pleasure shortlived
in my heart is real caring
      and the desire to give......

...... of oneself, to others
      who, in fact, deserve better
so, to one, I give it all
      as friends are forever!

And, in return, I wish
      for the riches in my path
more often than not, it never comes
      I settle for less than half............

......of what I believe
      is honestly, truthfully due
but, always in the end
      somehow, it falls through......

......to my enemies, to my friends
      even to those I've never met
but through it all, I continue
      and I ain't given up yet!

In my life is sometimes happiness
　　　but, oh, so much of it is sorrow
I ain't moping 'cause I am hoping
　　　for a better day tomorrow!

JAMES MONROE JOHNSON

"O N C E !"
(July 18, 1974)
Green Bay, Wisconsin

You asked for tenderness
    I was too strong
you needed righteousness
    I was all wrong
……in many ways
and many things

                You wished for happiness
                    I made you sad
                you wanted some peace
                    I was always mad
                …… many times
                about many things

You liked togetherness
    I left you alone
you begged for security
    I was constantly gone
……to many places
to do many things

                You loved me
                    but I couldn't see it
                you wanted me your lover
                    but I wouldn't be it
                ……for many reasons
                and other things!

"In Yo" Eyes"
(March 3, 1993)
Long Beach, California

I shall try and separate
    what I think
    from what
    I am supposed
    to think

        because if I really told you
        what's exactly
        on my mind
        it is highly conceivable
        that you may judge me
        based on inconclusive data

and that alone
may put me wrong......
......in yo' eyes

I shall try and refrain
    from re-living
    the pain
    of a past
    I wish to forget

        because I loved and lost
        self-esteem offended
        offered little, gave all
        and took nothing
        but it still ended

and that could prove to be
a lifelong liability......
......in yo' eyes!

41

JAMES MONROE JOHNSON

"In Yo' Way!"
(October 21, 1993)
Dallas, Texas

When you knew me, if you ever knew me
was I okay then?
did I say anything that you wanted to hear
whenever you said when?
Or, did you find me then as you find me now...
......just somebody in yo' way?

Were any of your desires ever satisfied
in any of the things I've done?
were you extra glad when you weren't awful mad
did I ease your burdens some?
Or, do you find me now as you found me then......
......just somebody in yo' way?

Did you do what you wanted to do
when you and I were together?
was my company where you wanted to be
or, did you wish for another fellow?
or, did you find me then as you find me now............
........just somebody in yo' way?

Was I looked up at, or down on
when you looked into my eyes?
was I being cuddled while my heart was muddied
or, was I just being patronized?
or, did you find me then as you find me now......
.... just somebody in yo' way?

Perhaps my words are meaningless
but what I said then, I still mean now
unless you are really capable of hearing

you wouldn't believe me anyhow
so, if you find me now as you found me then……
it wouldn't be too difficult for it all to end
…… unless I am just somebody in yo' way!

"N O E T I C I S M"
(May 25, 1979)
Gautier, Mississippi

Patiently, I wait

    diligently, I search

        defiantly, I am alone

and painfully, it hurts

Lustfully, I played

    uncharacteristically, I wept

        chauvinistically, I behaved

and naturally, I slept

Complacently, I loved

    oppressively, I fought

        introvertedly, I separated

and regrettably, I lost

Retortedly, I contest it all!

"And On And On And On And On"
(April 23, 1970)
Phu Tai, South Vietnam

At face value, I take it
forever the best, I make it
never but never, will I fake it
but on and on, I still lose

the best I know, I try to live
the all I have, I try and give
the most of it, always it is
but on and on, I still lose

wherever is erect, I let stand
whomever needs support, I lend a hand
whichever is great, I think grand
but on and on, I still lose

what's not mine, I leave alone
which comes over, I pass on
when it's business, I mind my own
but on and on, I still lose!

JAMES MONROE JOHNSON

"Making It Hard"
(June 29, 1974
University of Miami, Florida

Here's Saturday morn
an unlucky guy
truck's broken down
can't ride

hot and humid
hard and dry

it's so hard
to make it!

Bar's closed
not even a drink
gnats pestering
can't think

waiting for a repairman
from Friday's brink

it's hard to
try and make it!

Feeling so bad
from the night before
got the "ass"
'cause my truck won't roar

thinking of leaving
but got no place to go

46

gotta sit here

and try
and make it!

JAMES MONROE JOHNSON

"I Have Tried To Fight It"
(August 5, 1974)
Racine, Wisconsin

I have tried to fight it
in spite of it
and I am not yet sure I lost

the battle goes on
neither right nor wrong
I yet wonder who's at fault

I have tried to fight it
without seeing it
and I am not yet sure I am not

the life continues on
sometimes right, often wrong
I yet wonder what I've got

fighting the battles
of a nameless personal war

trying to be something human
......within
really real!

"Myself — And My Heart"
(March 3, 1993)
Long Beach, California

Conversely, I feel betrayed
in my fifty years of living

that so much less was taken
than, personally, I was giving…

……of myself — and my heart

Systematically, I try and follow
what's considered the norm

until somewhere along the way
I realize where I am going……

……by myself — and my heart

Consequently, I will decide
at an appropriate time

that the ideas and thoughts of others
aren't necessarily mine…

…nor for me — or my heart

Responsibly, I have learned
in my new priority

what you do is up to you
as long as it doesn't concern me……

……myself — and my heart!

"Bellefontaine"
(August 3, 1984)
Bellefontaine, Mississippi

In the midst of the State of Mississippi
right on highway number nine
is the itsy bitsy town of Bellefontaine
I want you to know, it's the home of mine

I spent my whole life in Bellefontaine
except those few times I had gone
off to college and then to the Army
but, I always came back home

There's a lot of good people in Bellefontaine
the kind of people who wished you well
there's Samuel Mills and Buddy Hill
Joe Carroll Evans and Mr. Nail

In the heat of the farming season
you'll see tractors and trailers by the minute
'cause Bellefontaine is a farming town
just ask Gerald Knight and Jimmy Bennett

If you get lost in Bellefontaine
on highway nine or four-o-four
just ask anybody that you run upon
to point towards Caffey's grocery store

In the itsy bitsy town of Bellefontaine
population of 109
but, it's the hospitality of a lifetime
and I'm proud it's the home of mine!

JAMES MONROE JOHNSON

"No Can Do — Charley"
(August 8, 1967)
Qui Nhon, South Vietnam

The evening sun fades behind the mountain tops
      still the sounds of Charley's mortars
      never seems to stop!
A truce is called by our higher ups
all warring weapons are layed aside
still the hills and valleys are filled with VC
      Lying in wait with murderous eyes

there are wars and other wars
men have tried forever to end wars
but Charley keep crying: "No can do!"
He stalks the highways daily
he lay subtly for an American prey
but now we have ceased to talk so much
      to let our weapons have their say

The 1st Cavalry is roaming the fronts,1st Infantry Division
      brings up the rear
      helicopters evacuating the wounded
      and the dead
we all felt that the end was near
Our bombs are continuously dropped
along with our most effective physical strength
still Charley's infiltrating the South at will
      and holding us back a reasonable length

Peace-talks were often tried
      negotiations from all sides have failed
      every time we spoke peace to Charley
he vowed to send us to hell

If he keeps throwing those mighty mortars
he will do, almost, what they say
but we're gonna keep blasting with bombs
     until we drive his will away

JAMES MONROE JOHNSON

"In Thoughts Of You"
(February 1970)
Qui Nhon, South Vietnam

I hope you're happy that I am near
now, let me explain just why I'm here;
a silent voice is beckoning out of the blue
I stand here, meditating, in thoughts of you!

From fear of non-acceptance, I bear the pain
of my yearning for you, in total vain;
for anything you asked, I'd gladly do
as I stand here, now, in thoughts of you!

I try and blend my music to your desire
a touch of jazz and soul, my heart doth cry;
sweet meditated melodies for feelings anew
yet, I stand alone, in thoughts of you!

Young, and desirous I am, and pure in heart
begging for your acceptance, in full part;
why do you think I say these things I do?
why much I stand alone — in thoughts of you?

Thoughts of you are good, but they are blue
I need a lot more: I need you!

"Another Day"
(December 28, 1969)
Saigon, South Vietnam

May God keep you
safe, sound and happy

willing to smile and be sincere;

throughout your daily routines of life
for a purpose held secure

May He continue
to hold your hand

as you travel across the seas:

let us remember always to thank Him
and ne'er forget to say "Please"

May He feed you
your daily bread

'n plenty of warmth for your bed;

a steady hand to comb your head
a purpose in the life you've led

May God hear
the kind words you way

in every prayer you wish to pray;

'n every beat your heart display
and your pleas for "another day!"

"Everything"
(March 6, 1998)
Starkville, Mississippi

I've got everything......
to live for

and nothing for dying

everything to gain
and can lose nothing

for trying

it's not befitting
my ever quitting

'cause I've got everything

when I had no problems
to try and solve

unknown was my incentive
known but to God

then, He blessed me
by setting me free

'n now, I have everything

and among my blessings
is an optimistic will

to stay alive and healthy
while enjoying life's thrills
so, if I falter
in my lustful bliss
there shouldn't be anything
in this life I missed…
'cause I had everything!

"A Prayer In The Jungle"
(October 24, 1969)
Saigon, South Vietnam

The valleys are full of the enemy
    the fields are bedded in green rice
the tables are set with cans of c-rations
    and my clothes are eaten by mice

Leeches are crawling all over me
    the mosquitoes are humming like bees
my boots are torn from sharpened bamboo
    and snakes are striking from trees

Ants are building huge anthills
    scorpions are settling for one last bite
my ankles are swollen from lack of air
    by sleeping in my boots at night

My face is scratched and scarred to hell
    my arms are full of skin-burns and rash
my head is shaven because hair won't grow
    and on my forehead is a bayonet gash

These are only some of the things I have to do
    by being a soldier, I have to pull through
I pray to God, please let it be
    that I can live to face the enemy

It's not because of Charley that I am afraid
    but, it's the other enemies that want me dead
and, if it hadn't been for prayer that set the pace
    I would've give all up and died the first day

So, if anyone should say something good of this war
hear not his words and bid him farewell
unless you're been here, you'll never really know
the things we go through, 'cause "war is hell!"

"There's My Prayer"
(October 24, 1967)
Saigon, South Vietnam

For God so loved man
He made him whole

that he should follow Him
with a sinless soul

For man so loved God
he follows His desire

for fear of facing
that eternal fire

For God leads man
to an everlasting life beyond

when all fulfillments here on earth
will have been done

Then man hears the Lord
but fails to obey

and meets the flame of Satan
on Judgment Day!

JAMES MONROE JOHNSON

"Love Is Blind"
(October 28, 1967)
Saigon, South Vietnam

Love is beautiful; prettier than life
             love is a power frequented against time;

    Love is a feeling — a painful feeling, it is

        love is everything: Love is blind!

Love is strong, yet, so regretfully weak
             love is daring, yet, so understandably meek;

    Love, itself, is a damage to the mind

        love is everything: Love is blind!

How beautiful is love when love's so nigh?
             that powerful feeling any heart can supply;

    A feeling of desire that only true hearts find

        love is everything: Love is blind!

Love is something no one really understands
             it has been shared by many a stronger man;

    Two hearts true, together, a love is in kind

        love is everything: Love is blind!

"What Is Life — Without Love?"
(March 17, 1968)
Fort Benning, Georgia

What is a man when he's alone?
what is a child without a home?
what is God without the Heavens above?
what is life — without love?

What is femininity without female grace?
what is masculinity without a man's face?
what is a star without the sky above?
what is life — without love?

What is music when there're no instruments?
what is satisfaction without content?
what is a bird without his lady dove?
what is live — without love?

What is appetizing when there's no food?
what is sadness when there's no mood?
what good is an insert without a glove?
what is life — without love?

What is trust without faith?
what is icing when it's not on the cake?
what is thinking when nothing's thought of?
what is life — without love?

JAMES MONROE JOHNSON

"All Messed Up"
(April 13, 1967)
Fort Benning, Georgia

I climbed the door
and shut the stairs

I said my clothes
and pulled off my prayers

I turned off the bed
and got into the light
just because I'm thinking
of you tonight!

I got out of the stairs
and went down the bed

to comb my teeth
and brush my head

I came in through the breakfast
sat down at the door
just because I thought
of you the night before

I got into the garage
and backed out of the car

I lit up the radio
and turned on a cigar

I turned on my horn
and honked my lights
all because I'll be thinking
of you again tonight!

JAMES MONROE JOHNSON

"Myself"
(February 21, 2003)
Starkville, Mississippi

I have to live with myself, and so
I want to be fit for myself to know

I want to be able as the days go by
always to look myself in the eye

I don't want to stand with the setting sun
and hate myself for the things I've done

I want to go out with my head erect
I want to deserve every man's respect

Here, in the struggle for fame and all else
I want to be able to like myself

I don't want to look at me and know
that I'm a failure and an empty show

I can never hide myself from me
'cause I see what others may never see

I know what others may never know
I can't ever fool myself, and so......

......whatever happens, I want to be
self-respecting and conscience-free!!!!

"Between The Lines"
(November 11, 1967)
Qui Nhon, South Vietnam

I was wrong, darling, and I am sorry
　　I must've disgraced you
　　　　many a time

I do feel sorrow
　　and now I am hoping

.... you can read between the lines

My heart won't let me say those thing
　　that I wish to say
　　　　that's on my mind

but, I am throwing
　　every hint your way

.... try and read between the lines

I know the right things
　　to say and do
　　　　when I've done wrong and wish to bind

all the hard feelings
　　between the two of us

.... if only you read between the lines

I feel so bad
      that I did you wrong
            I lied to you and you treated me so kind

you know what I am asking
      of you now

………… so you must read between the lines

"To Know Real Love"
(November 1, 1967)
Qui Nhon, South Vietnam

If you thought you were falling in love
how would you feel and what would you do?

would you try and reverse the process
and try and stop my loving you?

Or, would you let your heart lead its own
and take the course of love at will?

just let me know what you would do
I'd want to know just how you feel………

You see, I'd like to have you love me
love me for real and not be a flirt

I think it's time I had someone worthy
'cause I've seen love at its worst………

I can picture it being so wonderful
just you and I and the big wild blue

I would like that so very much, indeed
'cause I think I'm falling for you!

JAMES MONROE JOHNSON

"Me and You"
(June 28, 1974)
University of Miami, Florida

I listen
to your words

I hear them loud and clear

I watch you lips as the words
flow through
so true
to me from you

I hear
what you say

I listen good: Ears open

I feel the strength in your ideas
to connive
to survive
from you to me

I believe
your way of life

I understand your way of living

I know it hasn't been easy to do
being yourself
with everyone else

even between me and you!

"Something Evil"
(July 18, 1974)
University of Miami, Florida

Sometimes, I wonder
.... really, it these things are real
anticipation of goodness
frequency of badness
the conspiracy to commit
something evil

the ups and down of living
on the way up
falling down
desperation and dispair
contrast and compare all things
and people who inhabit
something evil

with all of the goodness
in the world
here, there and everywhere
from where does all the evil come?
in the blood
or the attitude?

it's evident......
...... and evil

"Strengthening Weakness"
(July 15, 1974)
Miami, Florida

Tempt me ....
        I am just that weak
        weak enough to accept the challenge
        and strong enough to follow it through
        be it that you are as weak as I
        or twice as strong
        before you tempt me

Weak temptation.........
        breeds a weak response
        remember the laws of giving
        it is but the responsibility
        that we all share, to some extent
        I will gain strength from your weaknesses
        if you tempt me

You have been tempted......
        you showed your strength
        you're dominated by weaknesses
        and they are but an outgoing trait
        of your character
        run to someone stronger
        you need their strength
        you'll never make it on your own

A strengthening weakness
        doesn't get stronger
        but weaker

"Raining Loneliness"
(January 4, 1970)
Pleiku, South Vietnam

It raining outside
    and I am chills
        I need your arms to comfort me;
help me dear, I am lonely without you
Oh! How much hurt can loneliness be?

With each fallen raindrop I feel the need for you
        torn from the depths of my heart;
with each shallow splash of dripping water
I feel I'm losing another part!

When rain clouds form high, dark and overhead
        deep within, my heartbeats fray;
because I am here and I am lonely
raining loneliness marks my day!

Only God knows the final ending
        the when, where and how of it all;
I constantly ask and sincerely pray
you're beside me when I fall!

The sound of the raindrops on the rooftops
        it melodic, symphonic and sweet;
if it were not for loneliness in my heart
the sweetest of music, they would be!

The clouds are parting, sunrays are prying through
        a beautiful rainbow lay to the east;
an April shower has washed me a new
meaning of loneliness known only to me!

JAMES MONROE JOHNSON

Raining loneliness! Rain purple raindrops
       wash upon my face the grace of life:
I accept the cleanliness of your purity
and shed a tear as my sacrifice!

"U T O P I A"
(November 6, 1993)
Eupora, Mississippi

If everyone in the world
were just like me
such a beautiful place this world would be

Everyone would be happy
there wouldn't be anybody sad
there wouldn't be instigators to make other people mad

Every soul would be saved
everybody would have a job
never a woman would be raped, never a man would be robbed

There wouldn't be crime
rampant in the streets
not even racial bigots hiding under white sheets

Poetry would be appreciated
music would be fun
art would be affordable and nobody would own a gun

Domestic animals could roam
from house to house each day
and animals in the wild wouldn't be anybody's prey

We would all help each other
wish each other blessed
we'd watch each other's back and give one another respect

Not a stomach would be hungry
not a lie would be told
not a baby being aborted, no more stolen property sold

Every woman would find love
each man would have a wife
no one would go without
'cause we would all sacrifice!

Help me pray ……… for that day …… U T O P I A !

"Our Men In Green"
(April 3, 1967)
Cam Ranh Bay, South Vietnam

I am lonely on the battlefields of war
    war is a lonely and hazardous trade
        from it are inflictions of many pains
    the cost is high — all matters essayed

    On the battlefields of the darkened front
weapons in hand, fear heavily on the mind
    propaganda pleads for total beliefs
our man in green, the noted kind

Pure in compassion, faith in God
    blessed with life and freedom bold
        fighting seven years for not himself
    but for his people and a nation whole

    Stand firm, young soldier, carry your shield
        with your sword in hand, march and stay
            keep in unison, the steps of patriotism
let not democracy fade away

I come to your aid, bloody hands are mine
    I fight hand and I am without rest
        from the fields of battle, we lay firm
our men in green, preserving conquest!

"!A Feeling At Heart!"
(November 5, 1972)
Miami, Florida

In my heart

    something good I feel

    a different feeling, and so real
when I can explain, then I will

but there's something nice …… in my heart!

With my attitude

    I really should be ashamed

    even to myself, I can't explain
who, but you, can I blame?

for this something nice ……… in my heart!

To this point

    if you would only believe

    a heavy heart would be relieved
and a new relationship could be conceived

… out of this something nice …… in my heart!

"Where Are We?"
(January 9, 1968)
Qui Nhon, South Vietnam

Where is the victorious one
in a peaceful way?
who is the transgressor
and what is the cost?

How many dollars are spent
on a needless cause?
how many lives are lost
in every battle we fought?

Where did it begin for us
who knows when it'll end?
haven't we paid the price already
when will disarmament begin?

Where are the originators
what do they hope to win?
what is our conflict here
and how did we get in?

Where are the negotiators
what's happened to the peace-talks?
why are we fighting and dying
in a war that's not our fault?

Help us, O God, give us peace
for we know not, "Where Are We!"

JAMES MONROE JOHNSON

"For America, It is"
(April 3, 1967)
Saigon, South Vietnam

My day is long and hard
        but still I work
continuously from sunrise
           to sunset
I leave not a task
        until the job is done
I must work on
        until agreements are met

I am a soldier,
        born and bred on American soil
and I offered my services
        to my country first
without peace in the world
        home is never safe
I yearn for surrender
        of the enemy's thirst

I gave to my country
        my first allegiance
to the combat zone
        I journeyed at will
without freedom here,
        I have none at home
damnation to any aggressor
        this I feel

My hours are restless
              little time I sleep
I think daily of
              the American dream
Across the ocean,
              o'er the horizon, I share
the radiant light
              of freedom's beam

Let the big bell chime, let the green flowers grow
let the freedom songs sing "America," and the world's democracies
grow!

JAMES MONROE JOHNSON

"It Ain't A Dream!"
(July 8, 1993)
Starkville, Mississippi

Startled, I was, then pinching myself
    inside, I felt awfully cheap

then I realized I was not the prize
    when I noticed I was not asleep

at the outset, it sounded romantic
    on the surface, nothing changed

then I realized I was not the prize
    when I began to notice the pain

disappointed I am, bewildered I must
    as my pains and sufferings engulf me

when I realized I was not the prize
    how can she do these things to me?

Excited, I was, so bemoaningful, too
    my ole ticker peaked, it seemed

when I realized I was not the prize
    how can one woman be so mean?

hard, at first, it was
    I had my moves resoundingly strong

then I was shaken when I was awakened
    and realized I was alone

cursing my being, my vulnerability
everything about me appeared unclean

I washed my face and shaved my head
before I realized this ain't no dream!

"To Be Near You"
(July 12, 1967)
Qui Nhon, South Vietnam

I am feeling
the emptiness now
it behooves me
through and through
there isn't anything I wouldn't do
if, but for a moment
to be near you!

To feel
your joyous warmth
your pleasant smile
all emotions restful and
inhibitions at ease
to know that we are again
together
blessed am I
because I am pleased!

The loneliness is here
and it engulfs me
I need your nearness
to see me through
there isn't anything I wouldn't do
it, but for a moment
to be near you!

"You, The Feeling and My Dreams"
(July 31, 1979)
Gautier, Mississippi

Last week, you were on my mind
today, you were in my home

an hour ago, you were in my arms
presently, I am all alone

yesterday, you were miles from me
last night, you were in my dreams

this afternoon, you were my companion
together, forever, though it seemed

Innocently, you drank my wine
silently, you used my phone
deliberately, you drove away
purposely, you were gone

Presently, I think of you
and how I felt when we kissed

tonight I'll dream again of you
and tomorrow I will miss............

...... you, the feeling and my dreams!

"Anticipation"
(August 18, 1974
Miami, Florida

Having had you
in my arms
felt your warmth
infiltrated your charms
...... at that moment, indeed
I felt good!

Having felt you
at my side
kissed your life
stared into your eyes
...... at that moment, indeed
I knew something good!

Having known
you wanted me too
feeling quite happy
just being with you
.... at that moment, indeed
I needed it good!

Having needed it ever so bad
with you then, so good
without you now, so sad
.... at that moment, indeed
I feel good.........
in anticipation
of better things......
............to come!

"As I Am Love"
(May 20, 1979)
Gautier, Mississippi

As I am
love
I feel love
need love
......and could certainly
use love!

before I
give up love
I will give in
to love
'cause I want love
...... and could certainly
use love!

while I have
love
I want to
make love
keep my faith
in love
for the sake
of love
to be loved
for love
.... and I could certainly
use love!

JAMES MONROE JOHNSON

"With Every Rising Sun"
(February 2, 1994)
Columbus, Mississippi

Believing
in my heart
what I know
is right
in my head

makes me fearful
of so many
tomorrows

while I
make adjustments
in my head
what I feel
is wrong
in my heart
that allows me
happiness
in
every night's
dream

only
with every rising sun
do I find solace
and each day
I bury
a little bit more
of my sorrow!

"Wasteful Opinion"
(February 2, 1994)
Columbus, Mississippi

In my opinion
it is so wasteful
to be

alive and well

and doing nothing

lively

bold and brave

and doing nothing

courageous

competent and able

and doing nothing

competent

and

experienced and knowledgeable

and doing nothing

expertly.

Unless I do something

meaningful and worthwhile soon,

even my opinion

will be wasted!

"No More Bull in Democracy"
(February 25, 1976)
First Printing: Florida Courier, Miami, Florida

Brother, brother, check yourself
your style is betrayed
what have you left?

Sister, sister, keep pushing ahead
hold atoned your morals
keep fresh your bread......

Son, son
have your fun
but, stay abreast of life
'n forget not where you're from......

Daughter, daughter
widen your smile
go forth and be worth
you're gaining in style......

People, people
follow the sun
keep the home fires burning
'til your obstacle's overcome......

Folks, folks
if you please
bear the guilt no longer
get up off your knees......

let the man
hear the plan
no more bull
will we stand ...

.... in democracy!

"Maybe Someday You'll Tell Me"
(July 23, 1976)
Miami, Florida

Prematurely
I adhere to say
how bold I am
to feel this way
and if I never get to feel
how deep this "thing" really is
maybe someday you'll tell me!

Without precedent
I wish to know
...... how far am I
and how far can I go?
and if I never seem to be
any of the things
you first saw in me
maybe someday you'll tell me!

Regardless of time
I still do
... have the highest regards
and respect for you
and if I never really know
where we each came from
or where we both will go
maybe someday you'll tell me!

"......Perhaps, Something'll Happen"
(July 22, 1976)
Miami, Florida

All of my life
      I've hoped to find
all things sweet and delicate
      yet firm and kind

but, until this day
      it has been my fate
either a bit too soon
            or much too late

If there is hope
      please let me find
where there is happiness
      and peace of mind

but, until this moment
      it's been my luck
either play a loser's game
          or give it up

But to whom do I look?
      what'd I hope to find?
if there isn't something
      or someone to be mine

to what do I owe
      to such a petty life?
whom had I destroyed
         and how long do I pay the price?

It's in your song
        your life, your style
damn the consequences
                I'll play the game awhile…

……who knows, perhaps something'll happen!

"Single Falsehood"
(April 4, 1979)
Gautier, Mississippi

I am single
  and I won't marry
    'til the right girl comes along:

but, while I'm waiting
  I don't mind dating
    any girl I know is wrong

While I'm single
  I am disengaged
    unhappy, alone and free;

somewhere in this world
  there is a girl
    who thinks exactly like me

I don't seek
  the married woman
    but she's everywhere I look

'Cause all of the single ladies
  have a house full of babies
    and don't know how to cook!

"Febewary's Coming!"
(January 13, 1994)
Eupora, Mississippi

Ah heard da boss man say:
"yo' month's coming fer yall"
an' dat's when Ah got happeee!
der black histerie month ain't fer all
febewary's coming, febewary's coming!

But Ah knows da boss man don't likit
causen it givet me pride
o'er all dem yars we'ums worked
while dey's tearin' our hides

der black histerie month is 'most here
febewary's coming, febewary's coming!

Dis is the month Ah learns
where Ah really comes from
an' any o' ya niggahs don't know dat
den you is really dumbbb

der black histerie month is 'proachin'
febewary's coming, febewary's coming!

We'ums celebrates famuss black folk
makin' our ownselves proud
dat we all come from somewhar's else
but only us can say it loud

dat black histerie month is nearnin'
febewary's coming, febewary's coming!

Ah's thinkin' 'bout Freddie Dougluss
an' Martin Luthah King
an' Harry Tubmun an' Rosie Parka
it makes me wanna sing

der black histerie month is here
febewary's coming, febewary's coming!

"My Two-Cents' Worth"
(March 1, 1997)
Starkville, Mississippi

I ain't the smartest guy in the world
nor am I the boldest
I ain't the youngest guy looking at you
nor am I the oldest

I ain't the best man to holler
nor am I better to shout
I ain't the first man to come to bat
and won't be last to strike out

But, I am speaking my peace
putting my two-cents in
there's so much I want to say
I hardly know where to begin

However, I'll start by saying
how beautiful I think you are
I've been around both sides of town
and you're the prettiest, by far

What little I know about you, I like
though I know not many sides
my knees quiver like chicken liver
when I look into your eyes!

That's why I married you!!!!

JAMES MONROE JOHNSON

"Tumblin' Walls — On Top Of Me"
(October 26, 1993)
Eupora, Mississippi

Now the walls have come tumblin' down around me
it doesn't hurt so much
except most everybody says: Such is life!

Because I have dark eyes
they say I can't see good
that my descendants from ole Afrika, didn't leave me much to go on
like, I see but don't see and hear, but don't hear
but, I refuse to let them know that I hear real good
'specially when I ain't listening
and I see extremely well when I find black cats crossing my trail

that old song they used to sing
is become a mockingbird in my ears
trying to remember my roots these days
afore they tore down the walls
which put 'em tumblin' all down 'round my head
however, I am learning
that the more I find out about this here America
the less I wish I know about ole Afrika
'cause back there, back then, they were really free
free to own me, enslave my forefathers
and sell us all into bondage
to the white colonialists
way over here in this here America
where I yearn to know my people and have my people know me
why I have dark eyes, and light skin
but very little of anything else but pure human rage

afore they tore down them walls
many of us was awondering
where did our futures lie?
now most of us know just how far we can go
afore we run up against them walls
which have been torn down
tumblin' on top of me!

"After Midnight"
(August 26, 1974)
Miami, Florida

in the wee hours
of the night
and you're alone now

how do you feel?
it's long past midnight
everyone else is gone

what now …… do you feel?

infatuated and confused
or disowned and misused
left alone and sad
or subdued and glad
reckoned with and reasoned
or set-up and seasoned
glorified and good
or horrified and misunderstood

alone in the night
after twelve, are you brave?

where is your courage now?

do your words
yet flow
…… so harshly?

"Take Your Time, Because......"
(August 31, 1974)
Miami, Florida

...... time is precious, it goes on

        steadily, night and day
        it has its moments of fulfillment
        its trials along the way

...... time is important, to each of us

        as it never is the same twice
        for those of us who lets it by
        will find the remainder won't suffice

.... time is meaningful, differently, we share

        but only that time gone past
        patience is time not yet used
        and which time that doesn't last

.... time is disastrous, used not wisely

        this moment in time comes not again
        those of us that waste our time
        has little time left, all in vain

"Black, Poor Male"
(February 26, 1993
Long Beach, California

Since I became a man
I have long forgotten
the least memorable days
of my youth
and my childish ways

I had no problems then
that my parents
or my friends
couldn't solve

But, stand alone now
as a man
a live, intelligent creature
my problems are real
testing my resolve

On any given day
obstacles along the way
many I pass on
but most are too strong
so I live with it

Yet four problems
remain solid
insurmountable, causing scorn
I was born black
I was born poor
I was born a male
and
I was born!

"Until A Certain Change"
(September 11, 1974)
Miami, Florida

I am happy to know you
you represent the one thing I like best
it matters not what you call yourself
to me, you're still the opposite sex

I don't care about your profession
your job matters none the least
it matters not what you wear
I still know what's underneath

our thoughts and ideas may differ
even our minds may go and come
but, when it's just you and I, alone
I still plan on having fun

I don't care what song you sing
I don't care what prayer you chant
it matters not what you say you are
my interest lies in your pants ……

………… and, until you change that
you're still female!

JAMES MONROE JOHNSON

"A Few Reasons Why"
(September 11, 1974)
Miami, Florida

A lady
is forever
a
woman

but
a woman
isn't necessarily
a lady

An
idea
in a woman
remains
professionally

an idea
in
a lady
becomes a thought

a lady
is
romanced
a
woman
has romance

Gentlemen
prefer
ladies!

"I Will Not Beg"
(January 30, 1976)
Miami, Florida

I will not beg
                even if I cry

I'll hold on — alone
                to make it, or die

I will not beg
                even if I'm dying

I'll hold on — alone
                and keep on trying

I will not beg
                even if I'm down

I'll hold on — alone
                'til I come around

I will not beg
                even if you leave

I'll hold on — alone
                'til it's I you need

I will not beg
                even if I turn red

I'll hold on — alone
but I will not beg!

"......Memories of You!"
(February 9, 1976)
University of Miami, Florida

Having patiently waited
   for your return
 a most joyful lesson
   I have learned
 realizing, at last
   you are for real
 the days forthcoming
   I am to live...... in memories of you

Having held your hand
   raved your smile
 my having waited
   made it worthwhile
 finally believing
   in natural fate
 for more of the same
   I shall wait...... for more memories of you

Having kissed your lips
   held you tight
 my thoughts of you
   came out right
 having felt your body
   so close to mine
 I patiently await
   for the next time.........

.... for new memories of you

"Keep Your Reasons"
(February 10, 1976)
University of Miami, Florida

I see many reasons you might refuse
    and keep saying no
    to my abuse

but, nevertheless, you'll someday find
    your eventual answer
    is out of line
and that, my dear, is yours to keep

I see fewer reasons you might deny
    your true feelings
    and their reasons why

but, nevertheless, someday you'll see
    just how unnecessary
    it turned out to be
and that, my dear, is yours to keep

I see no reasons you have to refrain
    from accepting my offers
    to join me again

but, nevertheless, it's soon be known
    just how far together
    we could have gone
and that too, my dear, will be yours to keep!

"The New Morality"
(February 9, 1976)
University of Miami, Florida

Looking through
my window

a different world
I see

short on human compassion

and

violence in the streets

no helping hand

to

a

fellowman

only a bid to have

not desire to understand

and

it's getting worse

all

the

while

"Set The Record Straight"
(April 4, 1979)
Gautier, Mississippi

What am I waiting for

I ask myself?

why do I want her

she has someone else

what is she doing

I would like to know

why does she lead me on

I should let her go

perhaps, she is happy

being where she is

that's what she doesn't believe

what I have to give

someday I will find

a reason not to wait

and I will tell her so

to set the record straight......

.... at least, for me!

JAMES MONROE JOHNSON

"Unless Its With You"
(August 8, 2000)
Starkville, Mississippi

As old as I am
I would like to become older
as bold as I am
I'd like to be bolder
so I could always find the courage
to really speak my mind
to say what I really believe
whether earthly, or divine

to be free to always do
those things that happiness brings
not only having the gifts of writing
but having the voice to sing
sweet and lovely ballards
to the Angel of my heart
but, God, in His infinite wisdom
knows I would fall apart

because I put everything I've got
into everything I do
and all that means "double"
when its cause is you
and now I have a last wish
in my attempt to live
there is a little left in me
and I ain't got much to give

but, oh, the love I'd make
with the finest quality of time
I would give all of my attention
to that precious Angel of mine

let no one mistake my purpose
just let me do my do
'cause I ain't gonna do nothin'
unless its with you!

JAMES MONROE JOHNSON

"Way Back Yonder Then"
(January 25, 1991)
Starkville, Mississippi

Never a moment passes
that I can ever find
when the mere thought of you
doesn't cross my mind

Even all day long
and at night, you are there
it's all intended to show
just how much I care

If I could find an hour
with myself alone
I'd fight these thoughts of you
to keep 'em from being so strong

Though thoughts of you
put smiles on my face
I yet find myself wanting
you to share my space

I find myself imagining
had I met you when
we could have grown up together
way back yonder then!

"Talkin' 'Bout Freedom!"
(January 29, 1991)
Starkville, Mississippi

Chorus: Free - dom, free - dom
if you ain't talkin" 'bout free-dom
ya better git outs ma face

Lawd, I's workin' so very hard
wid jes' ma back and hands
I ain't workin' fer myself
I's workin' fer the boss man

[Back to Chorus]

I hafta work ever' day
in any kind of weather
all of dem is after all of us
so we bes' stick together

[Back to Chorus]

In der big house dey's talkin'
'bout nuthin' no good
but iffen dey knew what I's thinkin'
dey'd catch me if dey could

[Back to Chorus]

Yonder hang ma brutha
wid a smile on his face
he don't have no mo' problems
he's resting in God's grace

ma brutha knew dat he would die
in his younga days
'cause iffen he couldn't be a free man
he didn't wanna be a slave

[Back to Chorus]

"Can't Take It Alone"
(January 31, 1991)
Starkville, Mississippi

It saddens me

I want you to know

how it hurts to be so close

and have to act so far away

It's taking its toll

you must know

how it feel to see

and act as If I'm not being seen

I'm trying

to hold out

and I will

for awhile

but God knows it's hard

and I can't take it......

............by myself alone

JAMES MONROE JOHNSON

"In Knowing Hearts"
(April 12, 1991)
Starkville, Mississippi

In my heart, I know
      you've got to go
           to where your heart really is

and, in your heart, you know
      that you got to go
           'cause that's how you feel

You must know.........

In the beginning, I knew
      I'd fall in love with you
           'cause my heart was beating heavy

and, in the end, you knew
      what you would do
           'cause you were in love already

You must know.........

You know your heart
      but follow your mind
I have no mind
      so I follow my heart
but love calls us both

Yes, in my heart, I know
      you must go
           to where your heart is

120

and, in your heart, you know
     that you must go
          to where your heart lives………

"Heartbeat Of My Mind"
(February 26, 1993)
Long Beach, California

I admire you
for obvious reasons
but you will never know
what I really feel

because my head
won't allow my heart
to share these feelings
with you…

you recognize
my personable smile
as you lay a soft hand
on my back

your being friendly
as a matter of course
beckons my friendliness……

as my admiration grows
toward you
I find happiness
when you're near

you can't know
your effect on me
but, if you would listen
you would hear
……the heartbeat
of my mind!

"Thousand Legs"
(August 6, 1998)
West Point, Mississippi

Oh, what a lad you are
nesting in the sun
in what manner do you lay
seeming, all in fun

and while I work all around you
you often toss and turn
through the rays of the heated sun
I wonder if you burn

Oft times I believe you see me
you always move when I pass
and if I weren't always in a hurry
I wouldn't go by you so fast

though the summer will soon be over
I wonder then, what'll happen to you
will you be here again next year
or, will the winter do its do?

at first, I thought you pesterous
then, I thought, you too, need life
and as long as you do what you're doing
I'm not fearful of your bite......
.... nor your thousand legs!

"So Where, I Ask, Am I?"
(April 25, 1994)
Eupora, Mississippi

Finally going to bed
bypassing a shower
missing the light switch
knocking over flowers
lay on my back
thoughts in my head
thinking I'm in Heaven
then realizing I ain't dead

so where, I ask, am I?

I had it all together
'xactly what I'd say
even smoothed my moves
to justify my way
and one mind told me
that was no need
just be forthright
and sew real seeds

then realizing I wasn't dead
so where, I ask, am I?

Tossing and turning
rolling about
a conscience awakening
with a loud shout
for once in the game
I see myself winning
'cause she had me pegged
right from the beginning!

"A Black Man's Freedom"
(November 5, 1993)
Eupora, Mississippi

Dey say I's free
and I've been lookin' fer dat freedum
where is dat freedum? An' is it fer me?

In ole Afriker, dey enslaved my 'ncesters
'causen dey didn't look fer freedum
dey talked a diff'rent langword
but, as dem younguns grew, dey all knew
dat freedum was here in Umericur

Den the settalers came and loaded up dem boats
der black tribesmun sold weak kin for honey an' goats
such a long journay, o'er the rough seas
had all dem black folk cramm'd 'gether like peas
den dey reach'd Umericur's shore
FREEDUM, dey cries, slave no mo'
little dey know 'bout dey beginning
der white folk taut us religun, while dey kept on sinnin'
dat, dey say, was Umericur

As der years passed on by an' der cotton grew high
many black folk start runnin' afore dey die
some start readin' and writin', some others bagin to learn
freedum for der black folk begin to turn
The South rose up against the North
their way, they refused to change
everybody took warring sides
abolitionists were to blame
they said: Freedom was coming!

JAMES MONROE JOHNSON

The Emancipation Proclamation was signed
in eighteen sixty-three
giving freedom to all slaves
but enslaving me
my forefathers worked the fields
enjoying their newfound freedom!

"And That Ain't Good"
(August 18, 1974)
Miami, Florida

May I retain
all that's within me

to have as my secret

from you?

Can I remove
any doubts I cast

in your presence?

Am I forever
to assume the inevitable

when the obvious is my downfall?

Less I retain

all that's within me

you will know me

partially

...... and that ain't good!

"Man To Himself"
(July 6, 1974)
Key West, Florida

deep, deep
    in the soul of man

    he is many things
    a heart, a body, a mind
    young, mature, old

    and to himself
    he has love………

on the surface
    his profile shows

    many things he is

    some disgraceful
    others distasteful

    but to himself
    his is love………

above and beyond
    the skin and tone

    he goes a merry way

    seeking only to find
    peace in kind

    but to himself
    he was loved!